Philippines
the land

Greg Nickles

A Bobbie Kalman Book

The Lands, Peoples, and Cultures Series

Crabtree Publishing Company

www.crabtreebooks.com

The Lands, Peoples, and Cultures Series

Created by Bobbie Kalman

Coordinating editor
Ellen Rodger

Project editor
Carrie Gleason

Production coordinator
Rosie Gowsell

Project development, photo research, and design
First Folio Resource Group, Inc.
Erinn Banting
Tom Dart
Söğüt Y. Güleç
Alana Lai
Debbie Smith

Editing
Carolyn Black

Prepress and Printing
Worzalla Publishing Company

Consultant
Maria Genitrix P. Nañes, Philippine Consulate General (Toronto)

Photographs
Marcello Bertinetti/Photo Researchers: p. 8 (bottom); Philippe Bourseiller/Images & Volcanoes/Hoa-Qui/ Photo Researchers: p. 11 (right); Jules Bucher/Photo Researchers: p. 26 (bottom); Corbis/Magma Photo News Inc./Paul Almasy: p. 17 (right); Corbis/Magma Photo News Inc./Jack Fields: p. 25 (top); Corbis/Magma Photo News Inc./Robert Holmes: p. 9 (bottom); Corbis/Magma Photo News Inc./David Samuel Robbins: p. 17 (left); Corbis/Magma Photo News Inc./Albrecht G. Schaefer: p. 10 (left), p. 16 (top), p. 23 (top); Corbis/Magma Photo News Inc./Paul A. Souders: p. 19 (right), p. 29 (bottom); Corbis/Magma Photo News Inc./Nik Wheeler: p. 16 (bottom); Corbis/Magma Photo News Inc./Michael S. Yamashita: p. 25 (bottom); Stuart Dee: cover; Mark Downey/Lucid Images: p. 7 (right), p. 9 (top), p. 13 (bottom), p. 14 (both), p. 20 (right), p. 24 (both), p. 26 (top), p. 27, p. 28 (right); Martin Flitman/Panos Pictures: p. 15 (left); Bruce Gordon/Photo Researchers: p. 13 (top); Michele & Tom Grimm/International Stock: p. 10 (right); David Hall/Photo Researchers: p. 30 (left); Cliff Hollenbeck/ International Stock: p. 5, p. 8 (top); Jay Ireland & Georgienne E. Bradley/Bradleyireland.com: p. 7 (left), p. 22 (top), p. 30 (right), p. 31 (both); Bullit Marquez/Associated Press/AP: p. 4 (bottom); Nancy Durrell McKenna/Panos Pictures: p. 15 (top right); Stephen & Donna O'Meara/Photo Researchers: p. 11 (left); Carl Purcell: p. 21 (top), p. 23 (bottom); Pat Roque/Associated Press/AP: p. 12; Marc Schlossman/Panos Pictures: p. 4 (top); Blair Seitz/Photo Researchers: title page, p. 3; Sean Sprague/Panos Pictures: p. 15 (bottom right), p. 20 (left),p. 21 (bottom), p. 22 (bottom), p. 29 (top); Chris Stowers/ Panos Pictures: p. 19 (left), p. 28 (left); Flora Torrance/Life File: p. 18 (top); John Woodhouse/Life File: p. 18 (bottom)

Map
Jim Chernishenko

Illustrations
Diane Eastman: icon
David Wysotski, Allure Illustrations: back cover

Cover: On the island of Luzon, the Ifugao people built large rice terraces that circle entire mountains.

Title page: A woman proudly displays a tuna fish she caught with her friend in Tayabas Bay, on the island of Mardinique.

Icon: A coconut palm, which is sometimes called "the tree of life," appears at the head of each section. Coconut palms are used for their wood, leaves, and fruit.

Back cover: Pangolins are mammals that are covered in hard scales. When threatened, they roll into a ball and use their scales to defend themselves.

Published by
Crabtree Publishing Company

PMB 16A,	612 Welland Avenue	73 Lime Walk
350 Fifth Avenue	St. Catharines	Headington
Suite 3308	Ontario, Canada	Oxford OX3 7AD
New York	L2M 5V6	United Kingdom
N.Y. 10118		

Cataloging in Publication Data
Nickles, Greg, 1969-
Philippines. The land / Greg Nickles.
p. cm. -- (The lands, peoples, and cultures series)
"A Bobbie Kalman book."
Includes index.
Summary: Introduces the geography, people, weather, natural resources, transportation, and economy of the Philippines.
ISBN 0-7787-9352-4 (RLB) -- ISBN 0-7787-9720-1 (pbk.)
1. Philippines--Description and travel--Juvenile literature. [1. Philippines.] I. Title. II. Series.
DS660 .N54 2002
959.9--dc21
2001047109
LC

Contents

Pacific archipelago

The Philippines is a country in the far west of the Pacific Ocean. It is an **archipelago**, or a group of islands, surrounded by clear blue waters and **coral reefs**. On the islands, mountains covered with thick, green rainforests tower above broad plains and sunny coasts.

Rich in resources

For thousands of years, Filipinos, or people who live in the Philippines, have farmed their land's rich soil and fished the waters of the surrounding seas. Today, Filipinos are working hard to develop new industries. They are mining their country's enormous **mineral** deposits and building factories to produce goods for themselves and the rest of the world.

Many challenges

The Philippines lies in a region where severe ocean storms, earthquakes, and volcanic eruptions are common. These natural disasters, as well as troubles with the government and economy, have been a challenge for Filipinos. Despite these problems, the country is growing and its people are thriving. Each day, the streets and fields of the islands are busy with Filipinos working and having fun.

(above) A shipyard worker at one of Manila's ports inspects a load of apples from China.

(opposite) Two carabaos, or water buffalo, bathe in a stream near Legazpi, a city on the island of Luzon. People in the Philippines use carabaos for farming and transportation.

(below) Stalls with colorful umbrellas, traffic, and people crowd a street in the Santa Cruz district of Manila.

Facts at a glance

Official name: Republic of the Philippines
Area: 115,830 square miles
  (300,000 square kilometers)
Population: 81,160,000
Capital: Manila
Official languages: Filipino and English
Main religion: Roman Catholicism
Currency: *peso*
National holiday: Independence Day
  (June 12)

Thousands of islands

The Philippines is made up of more than 7,100 islands. Of these, over 2,700 are so small that they do not even have a name. Many are just pieces of coral reef or rock poking out of the ocean. At high tide, the smallest islets disappear completely under the rising ocean water.

Largest of all

Luzon, in the north, is the largest island in the Philippines. It measures about 40,420 square miles (105,000 square kilometers). Mindanao, in the south, is the second-largest island. It measures 36,537 square miles (94,700 square kilometers).

Lying between Luzon and Mindanao are several other major islands, including a group called the Visayas that surrounds the small Visayan Sea.

The Sulu Archipelago

A double chain of islands called the Sulu Archipelago spreads southwest from Mindanao. The archipelago is made up of hundreds of thickly forested islands, coral reefs, pearl beds, and seashells. The islands shelter hidden coves and passages where smugglers and pirates have lurked for hundreds of years.

How the islands formed

The remains of coral reefs, found in Philippine mountains, lead some scientists to think that the land was once under water. These scientists believe that the Philippine Archipelago formed long ago, when the movement of underground rock and underwater volcanoes slowly pushed the ocean's floor upward and out of the water. Other scientists think that the massive eruption of an underwater volcano forced the ocean's floor above the water quite suddenly.

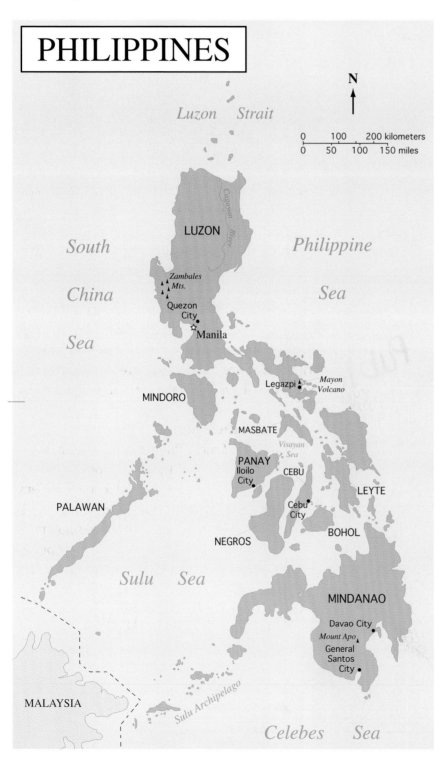

PHILIPPINES

Luzon Strait

N

0   100   200 kilometers
0   50   100   150 miles

South

China

Sea

Cagayan River

LUZON

Philippine

Sea

Zambales
Mts.

Quezon
City

Manila

MINDORO

Legazpi
Mayon
Volcano

MASBATE

Visayan
Sea

PANAY
Iloilo
City
CEBU

PALAWAN

Cebu
City

LEYTE

NEGROS

BOHOL

Sulu   Sea

MINDANAO

Davao City

Mount Apo

General
Santos
City

MALAYSIA

Sulu Archipelago

Celebes   Sea

Melting of the glaciers

Another theory suggests that the Philippine islands were once mountains joined to the continent of Asia. During the ancient **Ice Age**, gigantic glaciers, or large chunks of ice, melted, causing the Pacific Ocean to rise. Slowly, water crept between the mountains, and their peaks became the islands people see today.

(above) Tropical plants and palm trees grow along a sandy beach in El Nido, a city on the northwest coast of the island of Palawan.

Coasts and beaches

With so many islands, the Philippines has a long coastline — more than 22,549 miles (36,289 kilometers). Some beaches on the coast are sandy, while others are rocky. Large swamps border some coasts. These swamps are thick with mangrove trees, which are tropical trees held high above the water by their tangled roots.

Mountainous lands

The interiors of most Philippine islands have many rugged mountains, but few people. Rainforests, with trees up to 150 feet (46 meters) tall, grow on the mountainsides. Frequent rains feed streams and waterfalls that surge down the mountains. The tallest Philippine peak, Mount Apo, rises about 9,700 feet (2,956 meters) on the island of Mindanao. Like several other mountains in the country, Apo is an active volcano, which means that it occasionally erupts.

Most islands in the Philippines are very small. Only around 150 are larger than five square miles (fifteen square kilometers).

Rivers and lakes

Mountain streams flow into the Philippines' many rivers. The longest rivers are the Pasig River, which flows through the Philippine **capital** of Manila, on Luzon; the Cagayan River, which is also on Luzon; and the Mindanao River, on Mindanao. Filipinos rely on fresh water from rivers and lakes to **irrigate** their crops. They also use these water routes to carry goods and passengers from place to place.

Plains between the peaks

Plains stretch between the mountain ranges. They are mostly flat, with low hills, lakes, and rivers. The majority of Filipinos live and farm in these regions. They clear away plant and wildlife to make room for cities, towns, and large fields for farming. Two of the largest plains are on Luzon and Mindanao. Plains also lie along the island coasts.

(below) Farms, houses, and factories dot the plains near the Zambales Mountains, in southern Luzon.

(above) Pasajan Falls, outside Manila, are fed by mountain streams.

The Iyam River runs through a dense forest on the outskirts of Lucena City, in central Luzon.

The "last frontier"

The long, thin island of Palawan sits at the southwestern edge of the Philippines. Some people call it the "last frontier" because its mountainous and forested landscape is fringed with coral reefs and hundreds of islets. It is mostly wild and unsettled, but some Filipinos live here in large towns along the coast or in smaller communities in the island's forests. The forests are also home to monkeys, squirrels, deer, and other animals.

In the Tabon Caves, in the south of Palawan, **archaeologists** unearthed some of the earliest pottery and stone tools used by humans in the Philippines. Their most famous discovery is a piece of human skull that is about 22,000 years old. This ancient fragment is the oldest human remain found in Southeast Asia.

Houses with walls made from bamboo and roofs made with tightly woven palm leaves sit amid one of Palawan's lush forests.

9

Natural wonders

The Philippines is a country of geographic wonders, both on land and in the water. These wonders were created over thousands, and sometimes millions, of years.

Chocolate Hills of Bohol

The island of Bohol, in the southern part of the country, is home to the unusual Chocolate Hills. Hundreds of tall hills made of **limestone** and coral stand together, each in the shape of a nearly perfect, rounded cone. During the country's dry season, the hills become a rich brown color, similar to the color of chocolate. For the rest of the year, they are green with grass. Scientists believe that either soil **erosion** or volcanoes created the cone-shaped hills. Legends tell a different story. One legend explains that the hills are large rocks that giants hurled during a war long ago. Another legend says that the hills are enormous tears wept by a heartbroken giant.

Icicle-shaped stalactites hang from the mouth of St. Paul's Cave in Palawan.

The average height of the Chocolate Hills is 98 feet (30 meters).

Flowing underground

Deep in the forests of the island of Palawan, St. Paul's River flows through gigantic limestone caves. St. Paul's River is the longest known underground, or subterranean, river in the world. Over time, the river has carved its way through the limestone to create St. Paul's Cave. The ceilings of the cave are as high as 395 feet (120 meters). Hanging from the cave are large icicle-like stalactites, and pointing up from the floor are enormous stalagmites. Stalactites and stalagmites are formed from a mineral called calcite. As water drips through the ceiling of the cave, the mineral hardens, and the stalactites are formed.

(opposite) The Mayon Volcano has erupted more than 30 times since 1616, including a massive eruption in 2001. In Bicol, an ancient Philippine language, "mayon" means "beautiful."

The "Ring of Fire"

The Philippines has over 30 volcanoes, ten of which are active. The country is also surrounded by some of the deepest ocean trenches, or underwater valleys, in the world. Both the volcanoes and the trenches are part of the "Ring of Fire," a string of trenches and volcanoes that extends like a ring around the Pacific Ocean. The Ring of Fire is created by the grinding of tectonic plates deep under the earth's surface. These plates are gigantic layers of rock that are as large as continents. As they shift, they push and scrape against one another. The scraping is so powerful that it melts rock under the earth's surface, creating the fiery lava that pours from volcanoes. When the tectonic plates fold underneath one another, they create trenches.

Ocean depths and mountaintops

To the west of the country, the Philippine or Mindanao Trench lies at the bottom of the Pacific Ocean. This ocean trench is the second deepest crack in the earth's surface. It measures 34,218 feet (10,670 meters) deep, which is six times deeper than the Grand Canyon!

The Philippines' many volcanoes include the Taal and Mayon volcanoes, both of which are on Luzon. The Taal Volcano sits in the middle of a lake, and also has a lake in its crater. The Mayon Volcano is a perfectly shaped cone that towers 8,077 feet (2,462 meters) above the land.

Pinatubo explodes

For 600 years, Filipinos lived and worked in the shadow of Mount Pinatubo, a quiet volcano not far from Manila. On June 15, 1991, the mountain exploded. One thousand feet (300 meters) of the mountain's top blew high into the sky, raining rock, earth, and ash on the surrounding countryside. At the same time, a massive rainstorm battered the island. The ash and rain mixed, causing a deadly mudslide that buried entire villages, killed about 700 people, and left about 100,000 people homeless. Pinatubo erupted a few times afterward, but never as violently as on that day in 1991.

(top) After Mount Pinatubo erupted in 1991, molten lava flowed down its sides. As the lava cooled, it formed what looks like a river of rock.

Tropical weather

The Philippines has a tropical climate, which means that it is warm year-round. The country sits near the equator, an imaginary line around the center of the earth where the sun's rays are strongest. The only cool places in the Philippines are high in the mountains. Being close to the equator also means that, no matter what time of year, the sun rises around 6:00 a.m. and sets around 6:00 p.m.

Wet winds

Beginning in May, strong winds called monsoons carry moisture from the Indian Ocean, in the southwest, over the country. These winds usher in the wet season, which lasts until November. Heavy rains fall during the wet season, and the air becomes humid, or damp.

Dry breezes

Near the end of the wet season, the monsoons reverse direction. In December, they start to blow from the northeast. These cooler, drier monsoons begin the dry season, which lasts until May. At the beginning of the dry season, the weather is much less hot and humid than during the wet season. By February, the cooling monsoon winds fade and temperatures become hot again. March, April, and May are the hottest months in the Philippines.

(top) People walking and riding pedicabs, or three-wheeled bicycles, wade through knee-deep water after a monsoon floods the streets of Manila.

Typhoon!

From June to December, Filipinos watch for dangerous typhoons. Typhoons are violent, whirling windstorms that gather over the Pacific Ocean. They reach speeds of more than 60 miles (100 kilometers) per hour when they hit land. In the western Atlantic and the Caribbean, these storms are called hurricanes.

Twenty-five typhoons or more can strike the Philippines in one year. Mindanao, in the far south, is the only major island that does not lie in their path. Typhoons destroy homes, ruin crops, and bring rains and large waves that flood the coasts. Many Filipinos build their homes with strong walls and plant crops that grow close to the ground, so their homes and crops will not be damaged.

Earthquakes and monster waves

Earthquakes are a fact of life for Filipinos. They are caused by volcanic activity and by the scraping of tectonic plates beneath the earth. When earthquakes happen under the water, they can cause giant waves called tsunamis that smash into the coasts. On land, tremors from earthquakes loosen dirt on mountainsides. When heavy rains drench the mountains, this dirt turns into mud and crashes down the slopes in dangerous mudslides.

A village in southern Luzon is destroyed by a Signal 3 typhoon. Signal 3 typhoons, which are the most severe, have winds that blow more than 54 miles (87 kilometers) per hour.

An abandoned hotel in Baguio, on Luzon, perches above a deep gorge after heavy rains washed the earth out from under it.

The Filipinos

The Philippines is home to more than 70 different peoples. Most are **descendants** of the Malay, who came to the Philippines thousands of years ago from the nearby countries of Malaysia and Indonesia. More recently, smaller groups of **immigrants** have come to the Philippines from China, Spain, Mexico, and the United States.

The Tagalog

The Tagalog make up one-quarter of the country's population and live mostly in Manila, where they work in factories, banks, or other businesses. Some Tagalog also live in the surrounding countryside where they farm. Like most Filipinos, the Tagalog are Christians. Christians follow the teachings of Jesus Christ, whom they believe is the son of God.

Because so many Tagalog people live in the Philippines, they shape the country's politics, business, and arts. Their language, Tagalog, is the basis of Filipino, one of the Philippines' two official languages.

This Tagalog woman works at a bank in Manila.

A Cebuano woman, who lives on a farm on the island of Cebu, takes a break from her daily chores.

The Cebuano

The second largest group in the Philippines is the Cebuano. Most Cebuano live on the central island of Cebu, but some have spread to other central islands and to Mindanao. Many Cebuano live in large cities, while others dwell in the countryside, where they farm or fish for a living. Cebuano are very active in politics, trade, and the country's arts, especially music, painting, and sculpture. Like the Tagalog, most Cebuano are Christians, although many also follow traditional religious beliefs.

Igorot peoples

The name "Igorot" means "mountaineer." Ten main groups of Igorot live in the mountains of Luzon, many still following traditional ways of life. One group, the Ifugao, live in mountainside villages, in areas that they clear for growing large rice crops. Another group, the Kalinga, also grow rice, but they live near woods, where they hunt. The Igorot are also craftspeople who specialize in metalwork and weaving.

Some elderly Ifugao people, like this man, still wear traditional clothing.

Manobo peoples

The Manobo peoples, who live mostly on Mindanao and in the Sulu Archipelago, are Muslims. Muslims follow the religion of Islam. Islam is based on the teachings of God, whom Muslims call *Allah*, and his **prophet** Muhammad.

One of the largest groups of Manobo are the Bajau. Most Bajau are fishers. They live in traditional seaside villages, in houses that stand on stilts. A few Bajau even live on their fishing boats. The Tausug are another large group of Manobo. Throughout history, they were known as strong warriors. Today, many are farmers and fishers.

An awning made from woven palm leaves offers these Manobo boys shade after a basketball game in Cotabato, on the western coast of Mindanao.

A Negrito girl carries her little brother, who is wrapped in a blanket, through their village in northern Luzon.

The Negrito

The Negrito were some of the first people to settle in the Philippines, tens of thousands of years ago. Their descendants live throughout the country, including in the mountain highlands of Luzon, on the island of Palawan, and on the Visayan island of Panay. They practice customs similar to those of their ancient **ancestors**. They tend small crops for part of the year. Then, when the farming season ends, they live a nomadic lifestyle, moving from place to place. In recent years, survival has become difficult for Negritos. **Logging** and the eruptions of nearby Mount Pinatubo have ruined large parts of the highlands where they live.

Cities of the Philippines

Many cities in the Philippines are hundreds of years old, yet very few historical buildings remain. Most cities were destroyed during World War II, an international war that lasted from 1939 to 1945. After the war, Filipino cities were almost completely rebuilt.

Powerful Manila

The largest city in the Philippines, Manila has a **port** that sprawls around the eastern side of Manila Bay, on Luzon. For centuries, it has been the country's center of shipping and trade, as well as the seat of the national government.

Port of riches

In 1571, soldiers from Spain took over the site where Manila now stands and built a **fortress** there. For over 300 years, the Spanish ruled the Philippines. They used Manila's harbor as a stopover for their trading ships. These ships, which were loaded with silver and luxury goods such as silk, sailed between China and Mexico.

Huge containers of rice, which will be shipped to countries around the world, are piled on the docks of Manila's main port.

(top) Ayala Avenue is one of the busiest streets in Manila's financial district.

16

Parts of the ancient fortress and the walls which surrounded Intramuros still stand in Manila today.

Intramuros

When the Spanish began expanding their settlement in Manila, a small town grew within the fortress walls. The fortress town's name, Intramuros, means "between the walls." Today, Intramuros remains at the heart of Manila. It contains many of the country's remaining historic landmarks, including old churches, mansions, and government buildings.

San Agustin and Santiago

Spaniards finished building the impressive San Agustin Church in Intramuros in 1607. It is sometimes called "a permanent miracle in stone" because its solid walls have withstood centuries of earthquakes, fires, and enemy attacks. Nearby, stand the remains of Fort Santiago, which the Spanish built between 1590 and 1593. They used this fort to defend Manila Bay against attacks by ships from countries such as China, the Netherlands, and Portugal. Other important landmarks in Intramuros include Casa Manila, a mansion from the 1800s, and Manila Cathedral, which has been rebuilt five times because of damage caused by natural disasters and war.

Beyond the walls

The modern city of Manila spreads far beyond the Spaniards' old fortress walls. Not far from Intramuros lies an area called Chinatown, where thousands of people of Chinese ancestry live. South of Intramuros is Rizal Park, which is named after the country's national hero, José Rizal. Rizal was a doctor and author who wrote about the unfair way Spanish rulers treated Filipinos. Rizal Park's open spaces, fountains, and flowers make it a favorite place for Filipinos to relax and play. The business district and government buildings surround the park. Beyond the city center, houses and apartment buildings spread out in all directions.

The original Manila Cathedral was built in 1581. Since then, the building has been severely damaged by a fire, a typhoon, an earthquake, and war. The latest reconstruction was completed in 1958.

Quezon City

In 1975, Manila and some smaller, neighboring cities joined together to create the city of Metropolitan Manila. One of these neighboring cities was Quezon City. It was founded in 1939 by the popular Philippine president Manuel Luis Quezon. Situated in an area of rolling hills northeast of Manila, it was the capital of the Philippines from 1948 to 1976. Today, some government buildings and factories remain in the area, but it is mostly filled with homes.

Although it looks like a rectangular building, Fort San Pedro, in Cebu City, is actually shaped like a triangle.

Cebu City

Cebu City, on the island of Cebu, is the oldest city in the Philippines. Long ago, it was the site of a fishing village. After European explorer Ferdinand Magellan landed there in 1521, Spanish soldiers and merchants followed, expanding the fishing village into a trading port. Today, Cebu City bustles with manufacturing and shipping industries.

One of Cebu City's main attractions is the wooden cross that Magellan planted there. Its remains are encased in a larger cross, built to protect the older cross from people who chip off pieces for good luck. Fort San Pedro, also in Cebu City, was the first fort the Spanish built in the Philippines. It has since been a prison, a walled garden, and even the city zoo.

A crane looms over a construction site where new apartments are being built in Quezon City.

People, cars, and jeepneys, which are buses made from old Jeeps, weave through the streets of Davao. Davao got its name from the ancient Bagobo word "daba-daba," which means "fire."

Davao City

The city of Davao, on Mindanao, is the island's center of trade. Davao spreads out from the base of tall Mount Apo, and is surrounded by rich farmlands, mineral deposits, and vast forests. The city's growing industries are based on these natural resources.

Davao is one of the fastest-growing cities in the country. People from all over, including Japan and China, have made Davao their home. Their culture and religion is evident throughout the city, with landmarks such as the Long Hua and Taoist Temples. People who follow **Buddhism** pray at the Long Hua Temple while followers of **Taoism** pray at the Taoist Temple.

Iloilo City

Iloilo City is an old settlement on the southeastern coast of Panay Island, in the Visayas. Spanish buildings, including stone watchtowers and forts built in the 1700s and 1800s to protect the city from pirates, stand in the oldest parts of town. Today, Iloilo City is an important port from which the island's sugar crops are exported, or sold to other countries. It is also the center of a strong fishing industry.

GenSan City

The rapidly growing General Santos City sits on the shores of Sarangani Bay, on Mindanao. It is the southernmost city in the Philippines. General Santos City is named after General Paulino Santos, who led a group of settlers from Luzon and the Visayas to the city in 1939. Today, General Santos City is sometimes called GenSan City for short. Agriculture and fishing are two of the area's major industries.

The San Pedro Molo Cathedral stands in central Iloilo. The cathedral was built during the 1800s from coral rocks that came from one of the Philippines' many coral reefs.

 # Farming

Agriculture is the largest industry in the Philippines. Crops grow all year because of the country's warm climate. They thrive in the nutrient-rich soil, formed from the ash and rock of volcanoes. Filipino farmers also raise **livestock**, such as chickens and pigs, to feed their families. Some farmers raise cattle, but there are few large herds because there is not enough grazing land.

Common crops

Filipino farmers grow a wide variety of crops. These include vegetables such as **cassava** and beans; fruits such as mangoes, papayas, and bananas; and corn, sugar cane, and tobacco. Pili nuts are a crop that grows on trees. They grow in a fruit that is between two and three inches (six and seven centimeters) long. People eat pili nuts raw or roasted, extract their oil, or mix them into foods such as chocolate.

(above) Local farmers sell fresh mangoes, papayas, bananas, and other fruits at markets in nearby towns.

The rice crop

Rice is a major part of many Filipinos' diets. Farmland throughout the country is devoted to paddies, special fields where rice grows. Farmers grow rice seedlings in a field near the paddies. This practice reduces the time that rice plants spend in the paddies, freeing up the paddies for other rice crops.

Chickens, pigs, and cattle are raised on small farms throughout the Philippines. A woman feeds grain to her chickens on her farm near Davao.

Planting and harvest

To prepare paddies for the seedlings, farmers flood them with water using pumps, canals, ditches, and even buckets that they carry. Walls called dikes hold the water in the paddies. Then, farmers plow the flooded paddies with the help of strong animals called carabaos, and transplant the seedlings into the paddies by hand.

Once the plants are tall and turn a golden color, farmers open the dikes and drain the paddies. They cut the plants by hand, gathering and tying them in bundles. They leave these bundles in the paddies to dry in the sun. Later, the rice grains, which can be eaten, are separated from the rest of the plant, called the straw. Farmers feed the straw to livestock or use it to cover the roofs of their homes.

(below) Piles of rice are laid in the sun to dry. When the rice dries, it will be gathered up and taken to a processing plant, where it will be washed and bagged.

(above) A farmer picks rice seedlings from a flooded paddy near San Carlos, in central Luzon.

Banaue rice terraces

The Ifugao people of northern Luzon grow rice in the mountains, on the flat tops of the Banaue rice terraces. These terraces look like giant steps climbing the mountainsides. Some terraces are 4,920 feet (1,500 meters) high! The ancestors of the Ifugao began building the terraces about 3,000 years ago. With only simple tools and their hands, they slowly constructed each terrace step from rock and soil. Today, the terraces encircle entire mountains, covering 4,000 square miles (10,360 square kilometers).

Coconut king

The Philippines is one of the world's leading growers of coconuts. Coconuts grow in bunches near the top of coconut palm trees, which stand up to 100 feet (30 meters) tall. To harvest the coconuts, a picker climbs almost all the way up the tree's long, branchless trunk, often barefoot to get a better grip. Then, the picker cuts the coconuts free with a knife attached to a pole. The coconut's thick, green husk, or shell, cushions the fruit as it falls to the ground.

The "tree of life"

A coconut palm has so many uses that Filipinos sometimes call it the "tree of life." Builders use its wood and leaves as construction materials. Craftspeople make bowls and other items from coconut husks. Some Filipinos also burn the husks for fuel. Many drink the sweet milk inside the coconut's hard inner shell, and eat its white meat either raw or cooked. The meat is also dried to make copra. Oil squeezed from copra is used for cooking and to make soap, candles, and other household products.

(above) In 1995, the United Nations Educational, Scientific, and Cultural Organization (UNESCO) declared the Banaue rice terraces a World Heritage Site, a site of great cultural importance that should be protected.

To dry, cook, or press coconuts to make oil, people first have to remove the meat from coconuts' husks.

Sugar farming

Sugar comes from a plant called sugar cane. Chinese traders and settlers introduced sugar cane to the Philippines centuries ago. Later, Spaniards in the Philippines grew sugar cane on large farms called *haciendas*.

Most sugar cane is still grown on large farms. Workers harvest the long stalks of sugar cane by hand. Once they cut it, the cane is taken to a sugar mill where it is washed and then crushed to draw out its sweet juice. The juice is cooked and separated into sugar and a dark liquid called molasses. People use molasses in baking and to make an alcoholic drink called rum.

A worker collects long stalks of sugar cane at a **hacienda** *on the island of Negros.*

The gentle carabao

Without carabaos, Filipinos could not do much of their farm work. These water buffalo pull plows, carts, and other machines that farmers use. Carabaos are especially well suited to plowing flooded rice paddies because they are very strong, and unlike horses or oxen, they have wide hoofs that do not get stuck in the mud. Surprisingly, these large, slow animals are great swimmers! Some people even cross rivers by standing on the back of swimming carabaos.

From the sea

Seas, lakes, and rivers in the Philippines teem with fish. For hundreds of years, Filipinos have relied on fish as a source of food, and craftspeople have used materials from sea animals, such as the shells of oysters and tortoises, in their work.

Fresh from the sea

Thousands of fishing boats set out in Philippine waters daily. Fishers on big boats haul in large amounts of fish to sell at home or abroad. Fishers in small boats catch just enough to feed their families. Main catches include milkfish, tuna, anchovy, sardine, grouper, and snapper. Most Filipino fishers use nets, but some use spears, spear guns, traps, harpoons, and lures. At night, fishers use the light of lanterns to attract fish to the water's surface.

Freshly caught fish are lined up on flat bamboo mats that are stacked in piles. The fish are left in the sun to dry.

(above) Seaweed grows in the Celebes Sea, west of Mindanao. Once the seaweed is harvested, it is dried and eaten.

More than food

The waters surrounding the Philippines hold thousands of kinds of seashells, more kinds than anywhere in the world. They range from the pea shell, which is as small as a pea, to the giant clam shell, which is the world's largest shell. Filipinos decorate crafts and precious jewelry with these shells, or they sell them as souvenirs. They also make ornaments such as hair combs with the shell of another animal that swims in the water, the tortoise.

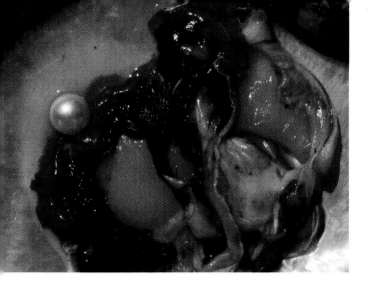

Oysters are caught and cleaned to remove the meat, pearl, and mother-of-pearl inside them. People eat the meat, use the pearls to make jewelry, and use the mother-of-pearl to decorate crafts and buttons.

Pearly white

Oysters in the Philippine seas are sources of valuable white or **iridescent** pearls, as well as mother-of-pearl. An oyster creates a pearl when a grain of sand or another particle gets lodged inside its shell. This particle irritates the oyster. To make the particle less uncomfortable, the oyster coats it with layers of a very smooth substance, eventually forming a round pearl. This smooth substance, called mother-of-pearl, also lines the inside of the oyster's shell.

Fishing traditions

Many Filipino fishers practice ancient fishing traditions. They believe that these traditions bring them good luck. Some fishers wear *anting-anting*, special charms that protect them from danger. Others cover their faces with cloth so that they do not scare fish. Another tradition involves putting food, such as rice cakes or chicken, on a raft and sending it to sea. This food is for the *engkantos*, or sea spirits. Fishers believe that if the *engkantos* are pleased, they will send a plentiful catch of fish.

Filipinos have used conch shells since ancient times to communicate with one another at sea. A conch is a sea **mollusk** with a large, spiral shell. When fishers blow into an empty conch shell, it makes a loud, trumpeting noise. The noise carries through the air over long distances.

Some species of giant clams grow to be 4 feet (1.2 meters) long and can weigh up to 500 pounds (226 kilograms).

🌴 From place to place 🌴

In the Philippines, people usually walk, ride a bicycle, or take a bus to get around. Some Filipinos drive cars or trucks, but they are very expensive to own. In many rural places, horse- or carabao-drawn carriages and carts roll down the roads. To get from island to island, people usually take ferries.

Ships and boats

Ships and boats have been an essential means of transportation in the Philippines for thousands of years. Travelers journey back and forth between the islands on ferries, while fishers set out in boats each day to catch fish. Traveling by ship or boat is common because flying, the only other way of traveling over large stretches of water, is very expensive.

(top) The bottom of a **banca** *is hollowed out of a heavy log, called a* **tongili,** *that does not rot. The* **banca***'s arms are made of bamboo.*

Some **vintas** *serve as ferries that transport people from one island to another.*

Bancas and *vintas*

People throughout the Philippines use several kinds of traditional boats. A *banca* is a small fishing craft with a flat bottom. Bamboo arms stretch out from the boat's sides, making it more stable, so fishers can stand without fear of tipping their boat. *Bancas* travel in rapids and other places that larger boats cannot.

A *vinta* is a traditional boat used by Manobo peoples in the south. It is a light, wooden canoe, with sails that are often brightly colored. The sails catch the wind to help the *vinta* move quickly through the water. The Manobo use *vintas* for fishing and transporting goods.

Two wheels and three

Bicycles and pedicabs, which are bikes with a carriage on the side for passengers, are a common sight in the Philippines. Motorcycles also roar down the roads, sometimes pulling a sidecar with passengers. Some sidecars are large enough to seat up to twelve people, with a roof to protect the passengers from the sun!

Jeepneys

During the first half of the 1900s, the United States ruled the Philippines, where it kept soldiers and military supplies. After the United States granted independence to the Philippines in 1946, American soldiers began to return home. They left behind many of their Jeeps, which they had used as military vehicles. Filipinos rebuilt the Jeeps into minibuses called jeepneys. Up to sixteen passengers, along with their packages and sometimes their livestock, can squeeze into a jeepney. Jeepneys are easy to spot because they are decorated with wild colors, designs, signs, and ornaments.

Two-wheeled horse-drawn carriages called **tartanilla** *carry tourists through the downtown areas of Cebu City. These carriages were a main means of travel from about 1900 to 1970 because they were inexpensive. Today, people travel in faster taxis and jeepneys. The carriages are no longer allowed on most main roads because they slow down traffic and litter the streets with horse dung.*

Industry and natural resources

In the last 50 years, the Philippines' economy has grown to include manufacturing. Today, local and foreign companies produce a variety of goods, including electrical equipment, textiles, clothes, furniture, medicines, and electronic goods such as microchips. The Philippines is also rich in natural resources, many of which people are just beginning to develop.

Down in the ground

All kinds of minerals are found in the mountains of the Philippines, including gold, silver, iron, copper, limestone, and salt. The mining industry is growing, but very slowly. Many minerals are hard to reach, so the cost of building a mine and transporting the minerals is expensive.

Another valuable substance that people dig up from the ground is guano, or seabird droppings that have collected in one spot for hundreds of years. People sell guano as plant fertilizer.

Miners on Mindanao scoop up pails full of water and gold nuggets from a stream. The gold nuggets are then separated from rocks that were in the water and melted down to make jewelry.

The arms, legs, and back of these chairs are made from thick pieces of bamboo. The seat is made from palm leaves that are tightly woven together.

From the forests

The trees of the Philippines supply countries around the world with lumber and other goods. Narra trees have a rich, reddish-brown wood called mahogany that people use to make furniture and carvings. Rubber is made from the sap of rubber trees. Ceiba trees provide *kapok*, a cottonlike substance that surrounds the trees' seeds. Ceiba is used to stuff mattresses and life preservers.

Bamboo is one of the most versatile plants harvested in the Philippines. Sometimes called a tree, it is actually a giant woody grass that grows up to 120 feet (36 meters) tall. Bamboo's strength and the light weight of its hollow stems make it a popular building material for rural homes and for furniture.

Shrinking forests

Philippine forests are becoming smaller because of heavy logging. In addition to destroying the homes of many forest animals, the logging leaves mountainsides bare, with no trees to hold soil in place. Without roots to anchor the soil, this bare land is more vulnerable to mudslides.

Producing power

To meet the demands of its growing cities and industries, the Philippines buys oil, its main energy source, from other countries but it also uses coal mined in the mountains. Dams channel the waters of many mountain rivers through **turbines** to create **hydroelectricity**. Heat from the country's volcanoes generates power in geothermal plants.

Homemade

Local craftspeople make many of the tools, furniture, decorations, and other items that Filipinos use around their homes. They produce everything from hats, mats, and pottery, to boats and roofs for rural homes. Some items they create, such as shell bracelets and tortoiseshell combs, are sold around the world.

This family is weaving fans, made from palm leaves, that will be sold at an outdoor market in Quezon City.

A metalworker operates a cutting machine at a factory in Kalibo, on the island of Panay. The parts he is making will be used for a car.

Diverse wildlife

A school of brightly colored anthias swims through a coral reef in the Philippines.

Plants and animals flourish in the Philippines, both on the islands and in the surrounding seas. Deer and water buffalo roam the land; crocodiles and leatherback turtles swim in the waters; and bats fly through the caves. The Philippines is also home to a kind of anteater called a pangolin. A pangolin's hard scales, which cover it from head to tail, protect it from the bites of ants and termites, on which it feeds.

Coral reefs

Coral reefs surround the Philippine Archipelago, and even make up parts of its islands. The huge reefs are actually millions of very tiny sea creatures called polyps. Each polyp creates coral, a hard, protective outer skeleton that becomes its home. Polyps connect their homes to the coral of other polyps. Over millions of years, these joined skeletons grow into gigantic reefs.

Coral reefs are home to a variety of animal life. Schools of colorful fish swim everywhere, trying to stay away from stinging sea anemones and sea urchins. Poisonous jellyfish, including the deadly Portuguese man-of-war, hover in search of **prey**. Large fish, such as groupers and moray eels, hide in the cracks of the reef, avoiding sharks and other **predators**, as well as waiting for their next meal to swim by.

Sharks

Many different species of shark glide by the coral reefs in the Philippines. They include the mako, the hammerhead, the rarely seen megamouth, and the whale shark, the world's largest fish. The whale shark is so big that it looks like a whale! Whale sharks swim alone or in groups near the water's surface, where they feed. They swim with their giant mouths open, so they can catch fish and plankton to eat. Sadly, the whale shark and several other shark species may soon become **extinct**. Many are hunted for their fins, jaws, skin, and meat, while some die after becoming tangled in fishing nets.

Whale sharks can grow to be 40 feet (12 meters) long.

When a tarsier catches an insect to eat, it closes its eyes, puts the insect's head all the way inside its mouth, and then opens its eyes and continues eating.

Tiny tarsiers

The tarsier, measuring just six inches (fifteen centimeters) long, is the smallest **primate** in the world. Tarsiers live high in trees. They only come out at night to hunt. Their large eyes help them see in the dark, and their neck cranes almost all the way around to look for prey and predators. Tarsiers have a long tail that helps them balance when climbing and leaping through the trees. The tips of their fingers are like suction cups, which helps them climb.

The Philippine eagle

The large Philippine eagle is the country's national symbol. Philippine eagles are more than 36 inches (1 meter) tall and are covered in feathers ranging from dark brown to off-white. They hunt monkeys, flying squirrels, large snakes, and hornbills, which are birds with very large bills.

The Philippine eagle is also known as the monkey-eating eagle because it eats small monkeys that live in Mindanao's rainforests.

In 2000, scientists estimated that only 100 Philippine eagles still survived on earth. To save the birds, a group of scientists from around the world created the Philippine Eagle Foundation. The group's headquarters is near the city of Davao. There, they try to breed Philippine eagles. About 400 other kinds of exotic birds in the Philippines also face extinction because growing cities and air pollution have ruined their habitats.

Glossary

ancestor A person from whom one is descended

archaeologist A person who studies the past by looking at buildings and artifacts

archipelago A large group of islands

Buddhism A religion founded by Buddha, an ancient religious leader from India

capital A city where the government of a state or country is located

cassava A starchy root vegetable that is shaped like a carrot

coral reef A ridge made up of the skeletons of sea animals, called polyps, that have died

descendant A person who can trace his or her family roots to a certain family or group

erosion The gradual washing away of soil and rocks by rain, wind, running water, and glaciers

extinct No longer in existence

fortress A strong building or place constructed to resist attacks

hydroelectricity Electricity produced by the flow of water

Ice Age The period between 115,000 and 10,000 B.C. when most of the northern hemisphere was covered by glaciers, or large chunks of ice

immigrant A person who settles in another country

iridescent With colors like those of the rainbow

irrigate To supply water to land

limestone A rock used for building

livestock Farm animals

logging The cutting down of forests

mineral A naturally occurring, non-living substance obtained through mining

mollusk An animal with a soft body and usually a hard shell

port A place where ships load and unload cargo

predator An animal that preys on other animals for survival

prey An animal hunted or caught by another animal for food

primate A member of the group of mammals that includes humans, apes, and monkeys

prophet A person who is believed to speak on behalf of God

Taoism A religion founded by LaoTse, an ancient Chinese philosopher

turbine An engine that uses water, steam, or air to make it move

Index

1 2 3 4 5 6 7 8 9 0   Printed in the USA   0 9 8 7 6 5 4 3 2